Little Woodland Babies

Photos by
David Kenny

AO PRESS

Written by
Jessica Lee Anderson

To Austin Wildlife Rescue and centers everywhere that help animals. – JLA

In fond memory of Kelly Simonetti, Director of Antler Ridge Wildlife Sanctuary. – DK

All photos taken by David Kenny apart from: Michael Anderson and Madison Kenny, p. 34. Animals featured but not mentioned specifically: black bear, front cover; groundhog, title page; rabbit, copyright page; opossum, dedication page; flying squirrels, p. 4-5; skunk, p. 30; fox, p. 31; deer, p. 32; squirrel, p. 33; and deer, back cover.

This Book Belongs to:
____

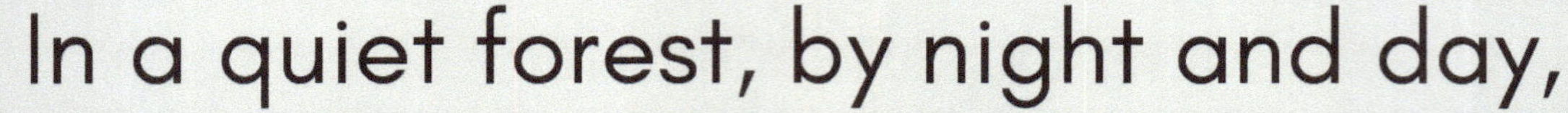
In a quiet forest, by night and day,

woodland babies roam and play.

Bear Cub wanders over,

sampling grass, nibbling clover.

Porcupine munches too.

Check out that wild hairdo!

Opossum climbs and explores,

crunching leaves on the forest floor.

Skunk Kit stomps and sniffs.

Watch out for stinky whiffs!

Baby Chipmunk skitters past—

those tiny legs climb so fast!

Fox listens to noises all around.

This Kit asks, "What is that sound?"

Baby Rabbit plays hide and seek,

1 . . . 2 . . . 3 . . . try not to peek!

Raccoon climbs up a tree.

Then shouts, "Hey, look at me!"

Groundhog finds a yummy treat—

tasty flowers, soft and sweet!

Baby Squirrel plays peek-a-boo.

A friend crawls up for a better view.

Cub steps with gentle care . . .

How did Cub get way up there?

Little Fawn learns how to stand.

Grass makes a soft place to land!

Growing babies need to rest.

They settle into dens and nests.

Little woodland babies, tucked in tight—

it's time for dreams, sweet ones - *goodnight.*

Jessica Lee Anderson is an award-winning author of over 100 books for young readers. Jessica loves spending time in nature and exploring the outdoors with her husband, Michael, and their daughter, Ava! You can learn more about Jessica by visiting www.jessicaleeanderson.com.

David Kenny is a photographer from New Jersey who enjoys photographing a wide variety of subjects, including reptiles, amphibians, birds, mammals, and landscapes. His images have been published in numerous books, magazines, calendars, and articles. David would like to thank Heather and Madison for their help and patience while taking many of these photos, plus all of the dedicated people who volunteered at Antler Ridge Wildlife Sanctuary.

Want to learn more about animals? Check out these books: